How To
Play Guitar and Sing
At The Same Time

The Amazing 11 Step Formula

Master the art of playing guitar while singing

This book is the companion to the **'Guitar Tablature Blank Notebook'** – 21 blank songs to notate your own compositions, available on **Amazon**.

How To Play Guitar and Sing At The Same Time – *The Amazing 11 Step Formula*

by **Rob Tutty**

How To Play Guitar and Sing At The Same Time

Contents

Join our community

Why not check out our Facebook group, for more tips, techniques, advice and guitar playing news:

www.facebook.com/groups/playguitarsing

Background

Do you wish you could play guitar AND sing AT THE SAME TIME?

Are you sat there struggling with the coordination involved, and find you can't concentrate on doing both together?

Have you given up and packed your guitar away because you think you'll never be able to do it?

Do you sit at home watching talent shows on television, feeling jealous of the latest young singing guitarist baring their soul on stage with a song they've written themselves?

Well it's time to stop watching TV talent shows for starters! Now get your guitar out, because this book is going to teach you how to sing while playing guitar. It could change your life.

"But I'll never be able to do it!"

Have you said this before? That's because you've been learning the wrong way. EVERYONE says they can't do something when they are doing it incorrectly over and over.

You've arrived at an obstacle most musicians have to overcome at some point in their musical life, and you can't see how to get over the hurdle.

It's frustrating isn't it...?

...you can play guitar

...and you are also able to sing (how good you can sing doesn't matter at this point)

But what happens when you come to attempt both at the same time?

It falls apart. You get annoyed with yourself that you are unable to perform a seemingly simple task that countless musicians achieve day in, day out. Does this sound like you? I know how you feel, because I was there myself once upon a time.

It's perfectly normal to struggle with this task initially. Think of your favorite singer/guitarist, and I guarantee they will have been here at some point. So already you have something in common with them!

Furthermore, just because they are successful, it doesn't mean they are better than you - they are just further along the journey than you are. Much like driving a car, the more you practice, the better you get.

The start of your journey...

I'm going to walk you through in baby steps how to sing and play guitar at the same time....at your pace, and in your time.

What we will be doing is dissecting the playing from the singing, and then marrying them both back together, to the point that you no longer think about what you are doing. Your strumming hand will become independent of what you are thinking, while you sing along.

And believe me, when you've got it, people will LOVE you for it. And your self-confidence will sky rocket. If you're doing this to appeal to the opposite sex, then you'll certainly be on to a winner when you've learnt. Everyone worships a solo singer/guitarist!

How good do I need to be before learning the techniques?

This book assumes that you have some degree of guitar playing and singing abilities, and will teach you to gradually join the two together.

However we will cover the first steps of playing guitar, and the basics to singing, just to help you refresh – you may even discover something you hadn't previously considered.

But if you do need to learn these individual tasks from scratch, don't worry. Even if you need to go off and brush up on your guitar playing first, you've already made the investment in this book so can just as easily come back to it when you're ready. There's really no rush.

And when you get there...

Whatever your reason for learning, singing and playing guitar together is one of the most satisfying things you can accomplish as a musician. When it all comes together, it is an incredible feeling.

Now just fast forward and indulge yourself in the future for a moment...

... imagine how you'll feel when you reach your goal of being a one man/woman band....and one of those moments you've dreaded arises, yep, you've got visitors to your home...you're in the kitchen pouring the drinks when you hear a voice from the living room...

..."ooo, I didn't know you play guitar", as someone discovers your acoustic guitar propped up next to the sofa. And you know exactly what the next question is going to be don't you.... so it's time to sink or swim. Are you ready? Then let's begin...

A bit about me

I vividly remember the day I decided I wanted to learn how to sing and play guitar simultaneously. But I remember even more the day I managed to achieve it for the first time. And what a feeling it was...I can't wait for you to get there too!

My journey began as a penniless student in a poky little room in a shared house with a cheap battered up acoustic guitar that my brother had offloaded on me. The strings were ridiculously spaced apart, and the neck was so thick that even forming open chords was an absolute nightmare – forget attempting barre chords! The gauge of the strings were crazily heavy, and took a ridiculous amount of pushing down just to form a simple E minor chord.

Yet it was this guitar that got me started, and gave me the bug to continue to learn.

Inexplicably, I managed to learn to play a few basic chords on this guitar, eventually progressing to playing songs...but without the singing.

As a big Oasis fan, it was their second album "What's the Story (Morning Glory)?" that steered me on to the guitar playing path. Around this time, Noel Gallagher had started popping up everywhere playing Oasis songs acoustically on the television and radio. It was a fantastic rendition of 'Cast No Shadow' on the Simon Mayo BBC lunchtime radio show that hooked me, and inspired me to want to progress by playing more. It blew me away that he was essentially a one man band, creating this amazing sound.

So I got hold of the Guitar Tablature for the album, and set about learning the songs.

The beauty of Oasis songs is that as a guitarist, due to the frequent use of open chords, they can be incredibly simple to learn. Bonus!

Yet to the non-guitar player, they have no idea how easy they are to play, so my housemates thought I was a guitar god.

After a few drinks, I'd get out the guitar and we'd have a late night sing song, from Nirvana to The Beatles - however at that point, it was them singing and me playing. Which is where my desire for something more kicked in...I wanted to be able to do both, and not just be the 'guitar guy'...

...so I set about learning to play guitar and sing at the same time. Like everyone does, I dived in head first, grabbing my tablature, and setting about my task. Big mistake. Needless to say, it ended horribly. My strumming hand was all over the place, and my singing was an inaudible, out of time drone.

Every time I tried to sing, my hand would lock up and lose any kind of rhythm.

The problem is, when you attempt it this way, one of the two tends to dominate over the other, as it's impossible to concentrate 100% on both at the same time. At least one of the two needs to be automatic without you needing to think about it. We'll come on to muscle memory shortly.

So I broke the task down, and sought to dissect where I was going wrong. There had to be an easier way. I grabbed my trusty dictaphone (remember those?!) and set about discovering exactly where I was going wrong, and what I could do to help myself get the hang of it.

This book takes you through my findings from the process, with a step by step guide showing you how you can do it too. I hope you find it as rewarding a process as I did.

Playing the guitar

Hopefully you have arrived here already a competent guitarist. And if you are, then feel free to skip this chapter.

Before moving on to playing guitar and singing at the same time, you'll want to at least be at a level where you know several open guitar chords, and how to strum in time. Anything more advanced can come later.

So if you're not quite there yet, or are a complete beginner, don't worry, we'll have a brief run-through of the most important aspects to help you. This should give you enough to get you started; the rest is up to you through using the 3p's....practice, practice and practice. It really is the only way to get good at something.

How good a player do I need to be?

It goes without saying that it is absolutely imperative that you are able to play the guitar well enough before attempting to play it and sing along at the same time. If any part of your brain is consciously thinking about the playing part, you will lessen your chances of success dramatically.

Throughout this book, I will be reiterating the importance of getting the guitar part accomplished to the point of second nature before going any further. The less you have to concentrate on, the better.

As long as you have some kind of basic rhythm, and ability to keep time, you will have enough of a foundation to make a real go of this.

Before you know it, you could be the next big thing to be discovered on YouTube!

Picking up the guitar

Now let's move on to the real thing. But before we start playing, you need to ensure you've got your setup correct beforehand.

First up...tune up

There is surely no worse sound in the world than an out of tune guitar. Ok, that may be an exaggeration, there are far worse sounds, fingernails on a chalkboard being one. But even if you're playing the correct guitar chord shapes in perfect timing, if the guitar itself is not in tune, the sound is going to be horrible.

For a guitar to sound the way it does, each string needs to be tuned to a specific note, when played "open". An open string refers to a string that is played without your fingers pressing the string anywhere on the fretboard.

So the six letters you're concerned with at this precise moment in time is EADGBE. Why? Well these are the notes of the open strings of the guitar. This is what you need to tune each string to, with the first E in the sequence relating to the top string (the thickest), and the last E relating to the bottom string (the thinnest).

Hold your guitar in the correct position - the thick E string is the one at the top.

The rest of the letters ADGBE follow the order of the strings down to the bottom string.

If you need an easy way of remembering these letters, try memorizing "Every Angry Dog Growls Before Eating". This is called a mnemonic, in that the first letter of every word represents a guitar string i.e. EADGBE. If you wish, you can come up with your own mnemonic if you find it easier to remember - this one was just some nonsense I came up with as I wrote this. I'm pretty sure not every angry dog growls before eating, but you get the idea!

If you have a guitar tuner, then this will make tuning your guitar far easier, however, you can easily tune a guitar yourself, and after a while you will be able to do it purely by ear. The easiest option? Download a guitar tuner to your smartphone from the app store.

Plectrum or pick?

Whatever you want to call it, a plectrum or pick (they both mean the same thing) is a small piece of (usually) plastic used to strum the strings of your guitar, or pick out individual notes on the strings.

You can of course choose to play the guitar with your fingers, strumming with your thumb, or finger nails. Personally I prefer to use a plectrum.

If you are a beginner, a nice thin plectrum is far easier to use, and will do the trick nicely.

To hold the plectrum, just place it resting on the side of your forefinger, just between the first and second joint (starting from the tip of your finger).

Then lightly grip the plectrum with your thumb. No need to grip it too hard.

Just practice a few chords, moving between them, and get used to the changes.

Getting clean sounds

One of the trickiest aspects of learning the guitar is getting each string to ring, without any buzz or muting.

What you often find when starting out, is that when you are playing a chord, one of your fretted fingers might be slightly touching an open string you are playing. The result is "string buzz", whereby you don't get a clean sound. Don't worry, with practice you can alleviate this.

Just concentrate on your finger placings, aim to get your fingers playing at as close to right angles to the fret board as you can, and ensure your fingernails are cut fairly short.

Long fingernails will inhibit your placings, preventing your finger from pushing the string all the way down.

Also pay attention to where your thumb sits behind the fretboard. It is incredibly tempting to bring your thumb over the top of the fretboard, because it feels more comfortable. It's a habit that I am guilty of. However, you lessen the space between your hand and the fretboard, and increase the likelihood of string buzz.

The correct place for your thumb is actually in the middle of the fretboard on the reverse of the neck. If you can start doing this from the outset, you will prevent bad habits creeping in early on. If only I'd done the same!

Of course, many guitarists have made a successful career out of having their thumb appear over the top of the fretboard, so the most important thing is to do whatever feels most comfortable for you. If that's what you want to do, and you can get a good clean sound, then go for it.

Hardening your fingertips

The more and more you play the guitar, the more you will notice the tips of your fingers getting slightly harder. Don't worry, this is normal, and is a good thing as it makes it easier to press the strings down.

When you are starting out, your fingertips are very soft, therefore making it tough to press the strings sufficiently. You may find it hurts to press the strings after a few minutes of playing, as it feels like they're 'digging in'.

Don't be frustrated by this, the only way to combat it is to keep playing and practicing, and eventually the tips of your fingers will harden, making the guitar easier to play.

Chords

If drums form the backbone of a song, then chords are the flesh on the bones. They define the sound and key of a song.

Without getting into a music theory lesson, a chord can simply be defined as a group of notes played at once. You don't necessarily need to know the theory behind chords - you just need to know how to play them.

You will come to rely on something called a chord box as you begin to learn the guitar. Chord boxes show you exactly where to place your fingers in relation to the strings, in order to make a chord shape.

Overleaf are the main open chord shapes, written in chord box format.

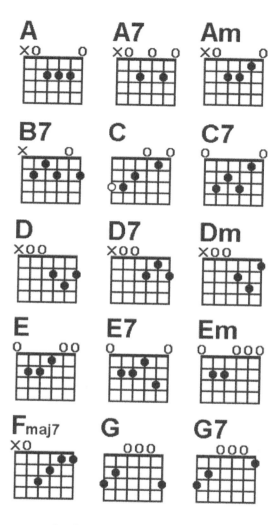

When you are looking at a chord box, the six vertical lines represent the strings of the guitar, with the "low sounding", thick, top E string on the left, and the "high sounding", thin, bottom E string on the right.

The dots show whereabouts on each string to place your fingers. Generally, the left-most dot will be your forefinger, and the rest will follow suit, wherever feels most comfortable. Often the dots will have a number written on them relating to the fingers of your hand – number 1 tells you where to place your forefinger, number 2 is the middle finger and so on.

When we refer to "open chords", these are chords that don't require a "barre" to be formed with your forefinger.

You will hear the phrase "barre chords", which refers to chords that require your forefinger to lie across the fretboard, pressing down every string, while the rest of your fingers shape the remainder of the chord. What this does in effect is makes your forefinger do the same job as a capo.

Guitar tablature

You may have heard of "guitar tablature" or "guitar tab" for short. It's a fantastic thing, and a god-send to anyone that can't read music.

There are those purists who argue that people should learn to read music full-stop, but if something makes it easier for you to do a task, then I don't see an issue. Personally, I swear by guitar tablature, I think it's brilliant.

Guitar tab is a simple system that shows you where to place your fingers, via a visual representation of the fretboard. The strings are represented by each line of the tablature. When looking at the tablature, the bottom line is the bottom E string (thin and high sounding), and the top line represents the top E string (thick and low sounding). You can remember this by simply lying your guitar down on the page, still pointing in the direction you hold it. The strings will correspond, whether you are left or right handed.

The numbers that appear on the tablature shows whereabouts on the fretboard you should press. For instance, a number 3 written on the D string means simply that – press the 3rd fret on the D string, and play it once.

These differ from chord boxes, so don't confuse the two. While chords are often shown on guitar tab too, generally you will see guitar solos written in tablature, giving an at a glance method of playing your favorite solo. You'll be the new Slash in no time!

Remember, chord boxes are usually above the stave on a piece of sheet music, while guitar tab usually appears underneath the stave throughout.

Overleaf is a C chord written in tablature:

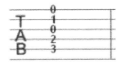

And below is 'Happy Birthday' written in tablature! Give it a go if you like:

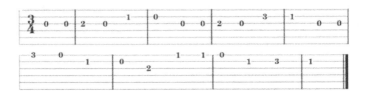

If you have a guitar tab book, you can usually find a useful guide at the back of the book explaining guitar tab in more detail. Make a point of reading this page as it's incredibly useful information.

Strumming

This refers to playing all of the strings in unison, to sound a chord.

Fret one of the open chords above, and with your strumming hand just play all six strings in one fluid motion. Don't seek to play one string louder than the others, just aim for one even sweep down through the strings, getting them to play cleanly.

Now play the chord over and over - begin with just doing down strokes, counting along as you do so. 1,2,3,4,1,2,3,4.

Then you can progress to doing down and up strokes, down, up, down, up, counting along still. Ensure your wrist is making the movements and not your whole arm. This will ensure more fluidity to your sound.

Playing songs

We'll talk about songs to play later on, but your priority right now is to play songs that have open chords in a straightforward, simple rhythm. Once you have got the hang of "easier" songs, then you can progress to something trickier with barre chords.

So to recap...

- Tune up
- Choose your plectrum
- Get clean sounds
- Harden your fingertips
- Chords
- Tablature
- Strumming
- Playing songs

Singing

There are a whole host of self-teaching courses you can find for learning to sing. We won't be going into these here, but there's a few general guidelines to help get you to a standard good enough to move on to the main part of this book.

It's widely perceived that singing is a natural talent - either you can do it or you can't. But anyone can sing with a few sensible preparations...

Listen to other singers

You will undoubtedly have your personal favorite singers that you listen to. So as you listen to their music, try and spot what it is you like about their voice, and what it is they do to make it unique and recognizable. Listen for techniques that you can mimic, or use as inspiration to create your own style and sound.

Foods

Believe it or not, there are certain foods and drinks that aren't great for your vocal chords just before any performance. For instance, milk is known for coating your throat, therefore stilting any sound, as is any caffeine based drink like tea or coffee. Aim to stick with water beforehand if you are planning on singing.

And if you are a smoker, then try to refrain from smoking before you are due to sing. Like caffeine, it can inhibit your vocal chords.

Warming up

Warming up is incredibly important, and should never be overlooked. It lessens the chances of you doing any damage to your voice.

Before you embark on a 'sing-song', it's always a good idea to loosen up your face first. Now this may sound a little weird, but one way to do this is by pulling faces! Honestly, it helps...

Open your mouth as wide as you can, then purse your lips, raising and lowering your eyebrows – just do everything you can think of to stretch those facial muscles. Keep repeating this for a few minutes, and your face should feel a lot looser.

Then try some neck and shoulder exercises, rotating your head and shoulders gently to loosen things up. Shake your arms to slacken them up too. These exercises will also help to de-stress you if you are about to perform.

Now give your voice a bit of a warm up by singing up and down through musical scales (e.g. doh, re, mi, fa, so, la, te, doh), or singing sounds such as "mimimimi" continually, or humming. Anything to loosen up the vocal chords is good. Just let the sound resonate.

Also try a "hot potato" sound, basically by imagining you've got a piece of hot potato in your mouth. Such sounds if done correctly can exercise your diaphragm, which as you'll see shortly is what we want to be doing as much as possible. The diaphragm is the place where you want to be projecting everything from. We cover this shortly in the "Breathing" section.

When singing your scales see how high up and low down you can get your voice. Don't do anything that feels uncomfortable – make sure they are notes that you aren't "reaching" for – the last thing we want you to do is cause any damage to your vocal chords.

When you reach your highest/lowest 'reachable' note, see how long you can hold it for, and mix it up with some other noises, preferably ones that will work your mouth, for instance "wah-wah-woo-wah".

You can even try speaking or humming the scales, using words or numbers as you go up through the notes. This will work out your vocal chords a bit more, letting the notes resonate, and allowing you to feel them hum within your chest and throat.

As you work through the scales, the vibrations of the notes you are making will let you spot where they vibrate the most, depending on the note you are making. This tells you where you are working your muscles out. The lower notes will generally resonate lower down, in your chest, while the higher notes will resonate higher up, in your throat and head.

Experiment a bit with how long you hold notes for, mixing it up with long and short notes. Just aim to maintain the strength and quality of the notes.

Another warming up exercise to try is "trilling" your lips. It's a good warming up exercise as the amount of breath you need to trill your lips is about the same amount you release to hold longer notes as you sing. Hopefully you know what I mean by trilling – making your lips vibrate while making a noise. Just do it when you're alone if you're worried about what you might look like!

Breathing

When singing, you are often taught to sing from your diaphragm, which you can find just underneath your ribcage. This enables you to have more control and power over your singing, as the diaphragm provides the support you need to hold notes and get more "oomph" behind your singing.

So as soon as you can, learn to breathe from your diaphragm, by making your stomach go in and out, and not your chest. It's tricky to get the hang of initially, so stick with it.

Just concentrate on forcing your breathing down, past your lungs and to your stomach. Feel the rise and fall of your tummy, and feel the muscles being used. When you start trying to sing, maintain this breathing pattern and start to feel how different your singing becomes with it emanating from these lower depths.

Don't know where your diaphragm is? Try having a side-splitting laugh about something, or if you can't laugh on command, recall the last time you laughed heartily, and what it felt like. The part down in your stomach that you can feel when you laugh like this is where your diaphragm is.

If this doesn't work for you, then try breathing out as hard as possible – the muscle you can feel when you do this is the diaphragm.

As you sing, just breathe enough air into your lungs to sing the upcoming line comfortably. You don't want too much air in your lungs, otherwise your singing can end up breathy. Gently release the air out as you sing, in a steady stream. This will help you carry a note for far longer, and strongly.

Eventually you'll get to know instinctively how much air is the perfect amount for what you are singing.

If you want to build up the strength of your lungs, you can do so every night before bed (or any time of the day if you wish). Ensure you are lying completely flat on your back (with no pillow behind your head), and spend a few minutes breathing in and out deeply, as deep as you possibly can. Let your stomach rise and fall. Then spend time doing the same with your lungs.

If you get into the habit of doing this every night, you will start to feel the benefit when you come to sing. You are expanding your lungs by doing this, and will gradually learn how to hold more air, and subsequently give more power.

Posture

Have a go for a moment at singing sitting down, in a hunched position. You should find that it's so much harder to sing nicely when compared to standing up with good posture.

Your chest and lungs need to be able to stretch comfortably – sitting down restricts them, and therefore restricts your breathing. Of course, it's still possible to sing well sitting down - Dave Grohl managed it when he broke his leg! Just ensure your back is straight and you are breathing correctly.

Your posture is as important as anything else when learning to sing. Your back should be straight, your chin upright, at a right-angle to your chest. Try singing the song you sang sitting down hunched, but now sing it with correct posture standing up. Notice what a difference it makes.

Ensure you always pay attention to your posture when you are singing – tiny changes can make all the difference.

Sing quietly to begin with

Try not to strain your voice initially – start by singing quietly to get control of the notes you are singing first. Then you can build up to singing louder.

The best place to sing louder is when you are on your own, and with no one for you to disturb, for instance out in the car on your own – then you can sing as loud as you like!

If you have neighbors or family that you are concerned about disturbing, you can always sing into your pillow as a last resort! It's best that you are able to practice when you can, so this might be your only option if there is a requirement to respect other people's peace and quiet.

Project your voice

To give as best a performance as you can, anytime you sing, sing like you're singing to the end of the room, and not just a meter in front of you.

Keep your head straight, look forward, adopt a good posture with your back straight, and project your voice from the diaphragm.

Pronounce your words and accentuate them as you form them with your mouth. Form the vowels and consonants correctly - don't mumble. When you're performing, your audience needs to be able to hear clearly what you are singing. So maintain perfect diction and project your voice at all times.

Have confidence

In a nutshell, don't be self-conscious, and just roll with it. Ignore other people's opinions. If you're worried about how good you are, just remember that with practice you WILL get better. And chances are you will be doing something others wish they had the confidence to do themselves. So show them who is boss, and give 100% to your performance. Make them jealous!

Record yourself and play back

This is a good technique for improving your voice, however you'll have to overcome any fears you may have of hearing your own voice. It's the only way you're going to hear where you can improve.

The key is not to be overly critical of yourself. Most people don't like the sound of their own voice, so just try listening to it a few times, so that you get used to how you sound. Then you can start to dissect your performance and note any good bits, and any points you can improve.

Practice

Predictable as it may sound, it is all about that word again. Quite simply….practice.

Here's your recap...

- Listen to other singers
- Watch what you eat
- Warm up
- Breath correctly
- Adopt good posture
- Sing quietly to begin with
- Project your voice
- Have confidence
- Record yourself
- Practice, practice, practice

Next, it is the moment you have been waiting for!

You are now ready to start piecing everything together. In the next chapter we will be moving on to the 11 steps to learning to sing and play guitar at the same time.

Step 1

Preparation - choosing your songs

The fear? Fear not the fear...

Many people approach singing while playing guitar at the same time in completely the wrong way, and dive in head first trying to do both at the same time without dissecting what they are doing. And the result? Invariably they will give up. You may even have felt like this yourself. So what's the key?

Well, firstly, do not be overwhelmed – it always feels tricky at first, but as I've said previously, every great singer/guitarist has been at this point. And some of them can't even sing!

Do you need to be a good singer? Of course not! No names mentioned, but we can all easily think of examples of poor singers that have made it big. Why do you think so many acts use auto-tuning on their voice?!

Remember, there was a time when you personally couldn't type, or couldn't drive, or even, when you were a baby, you couldn't walk. Think of anything that once upon a time you were unable to do, but since managed to learn. Remember when it felt like you would never manage to get the hang of it? But I bet you got there in the end? It will be exactly the same here.

Ok, so, pep talk over, let's get down to business.

Pick songs you LOVE

It goes without saying that the more you enjoy doing something, the easier it is to learn. Cast your mind back and remember when you were at school and you had to study books you had absolutely no interest in. Perhaps it was Shakespeare, or Chaucer even? Literary geniuses they may have been, but wasn't it so much harder to learn, so much more of a struggle to get engrossed in the story when you hadn't chosen the book yourself?

Now remember when you were free to pick a book of your choice from the library. Didn't your enjoyment just sky-rocket as you chose a Roald Dahl classic or the latest Harry Potter instalment? Your attention span no doubt increased, as did your reading speed.

It is the same with learning to play songs on the guitar. It is only ever going to be truly enjoyable if they are songs you like. In fact, scrap that, they need to be songs you LOVE.

On countless occasions in bands I've been in, there have been songs that are outside my comfort zone, and indeed, taste! And while I was happy to go along with them, they just aren't as enjoyable as signing a song you have a connection with.

These are going to be the songs you will live and breathe for the next few weeks and months, so they need to be close to your heart. Let's face it, a die-hard heavy metal fan likely isn't going to be happy learning a Lady Gaga song on the guitar...unless they have quite an eclectic taste in music.

So choose wisely. Take a few minutes to think about the songs you've loved in your life. What are you listening to at the moment? What CD's do you have in your car? Add these to your playlist. They don't even have to be songs that have guitar parts in them. Even dance tunes can be played on a guitar if you know the chords.

What we want to do right here is build up a list of potential songs to learn on the guitar. Some of them we will filter out later, as they won't all be so straightforward for us to learn at this point. I'll explain why in the next chapter, so don't worry about that right now, just concentrate on building up your list of favorite songs. You must have thought over the years, wow, I'd love to be able to play that. Well, add it to your list.

If you're learning this with the intention of playing to an audience/person, then it is worth bearing in mind that your repertoire perhaps should consist of well-known songs that many people know the words to. And here's the reason...

If you're playing your song to an audience, and things go wrong, you can prompt them to join in with you, and cover up the mistake. A quick "lemme hear ya" could well prompt hysteria from the crowd that Bruce Springsteen would be proud of! No one need ever know....all of a sudden that outro to Hey Jude doesn't seem so daunting...in fact a song like Hey Jude is ideal for its repetitive outro.

Any song you can find that has a lot of repetition throughout is great to acquaint yourself with as it will leave you with less to learn. If you've only got a few chords to learn, and they repeat themselves throughout, it's going to make your job a lot easier.

So seek inspiration where you can. Go through your CD/Record/Tape/Spotify collection, listen to the radio, and make a note of as many songs as possible that you love, and would love to be able to play. With the building blocks I'll be giving you, you'll be playing and singing them sooner than you think.

Open chords

Ok, so you've got your list of songs, now we need to whittle them down.

We need to do some research, and see which chords are involved in playing the songs you're interested in. The reason being, we want to find songs that ideally consist entirely of open chords, and even better if they are a repeating chord pattern. A great example is Songbird by Oasis, or Halo by Beyoncé.

Ideally we also want to find songs where the chords sit hand in hand with the lyrics. By this I mean a chord change occurs at the end of a sentence. Sometimes this isn't always the case, but if you can, find a song with regimented chord changes, that predictably change at certain places in the song.

In case you skipped the earlier chapter on playing the guitar, just to recap, open chords are the basic chords that can be played around the first few frets, and without forming barre chords.

The chords we are especially interested in are A, Am, C, D, Dm, E, Em, Fmaj7, G. If you can find songs with just any of these chords, it will help you immeasurably.

The reason being, the less you have to think about the chords you are playing, the more capacity you'll have for concentrating on your singing and timing. And while we're on the subject of singing, there's one consideration you need to make when you're selecting your songs...

Try to pick songs you KNOW you can sing and that fit in with your vocal range! The easier we can make this for you the better. Then perhaps later you can think about more advanced songs. Also try to pick songs where you know for a fact they get sung and played at the same time by the artist e.g. for instance if you've seen Ed Sheeran singing the song acoustically. This will help as you'll be able to find a rendition of the song they have done on YouTube, and use it as a guide. Find a version where you can see the chords they are playing quite clearly.

Of course, your favorite genre may not feature artists that play guitar and sing, such as dance music. No matter, you can still get the chords and put your own acoustic spin on it. All songs can be played on an acoustic guitar somehow...

When you haven't got your guitar with you...

While you listen to your songs, even if you're in a situation where you haven't got your guitar handy, you can still make the shapes of the chords with your fingers. Even without a fretboard present, you are still training your brain to recognize where the chords occur in relation to the lyrics.

Also get a feel for the rhythm, whether it's by tapping your foot like a metronome, or drumming on your legs with your palms, or nodding your head even. If you also aren't in a position where you can listen to the music, then Step 2 in the process 'Use your imagination' which follows will help.

Whatever your choice, we want to get the beat and timing into your subconscious. Anytime you listen to music, seek to lose yourself in it and acknowledge the rhythm in any way you can. Even to songs you're not interested in learning.

So anytime you've got a radio playing random tunes, try to get 'inside' the music. Slice it and dice it until you know what makes the song tick. Hum, tap, drum or sing along, whatever it takes to commit it to memory. But just remember not to let it affect your concentration if you're doing something like driving!

When you have your guitar with you, the key is not to overload yourself with songs. Take one at a time, let yourself become familiar with the lyrics, rhythm, chord changes and tempo. Then, you can allow yourself to try another.

So where do I get the chords for songs?

Some of you may be at a loss as to where exactly you can get hold of the chords for songs. Well, in truth you don't need to look far...

Your first port of call most of the time would be the internet. There are a whole host of guitar sites that have directories of songs and their chords. A quick search engine search for the song you want, along with "guitar tab" is a good start.

However, there is a drawback. The content on these sites is user-submitted and therefore is the person's "interpretation" of what chords and lyrics the song consists of. As a result, the outcome can be quite gruesome, on the other hand you'll sometimes find that the interpretation is spot on, but it depends on the user's experience. Thankfully, there is usually a 5 star rating system for each tab, which serves to indicate the accuracy of it. So make sure a tablature is accurate sounding before getting properly stuck in!

Alternatively, there is nothing better than having the official chord and lyric sheet or guitar tablature book to play from.

"Easy" songs

You may well have reached this chapter with virtually nothing on your list. Fear not, I've done some of the hard work for you.

To get you started, I have put together a list of well-known songs that have simple chord structures, which you can find in the Facebook group at www.facebook.com/groups/playguitarsing. I show you the best way I have found to approach these songs when learning them, so don't worry too much if you struggle to pick some suitable songs.

In the meantime, you can still work on your rhythm. Below are some great chord sequences that you can find in many popular songs. So anytime you feel like you just want to give your guitar playing a bit of a workout, play around with the chord sequences below.

We cover some of these in the songwriting section of this book....you never know, you may even end up coming up with a bit of a tune to go over the top of them, ready for your talent show debut...

- G, C, D
- G, Em, C, D
- A, E, D
- C, Fmaj7, Am, D7
- Am, C, G, D

Your quick recap...

- Make a list - pick songs you love
- Filter - keep the songs with an easy rhythm and open chords
- Source the sheet music/tablature

Time for a quick break

Right, you've made it through step 1, the preparation - so well done. Let's take a time-out (no caffeine, milk or cigarettes!), as things are about to get a little more serious...but in a good way of course...

Following are the remaining ten steps to achieving your goal of singing and playing guitar at the same time. You'll know by now that we're not going to dive straight in and just start trying to do both. You've got to learn the singing, then the playing, then slowly intertwine the two.

So hold tight, follow these exercises and you'll be in much, much better shape. There will come a time when you come to learn a new song that you won't need to follow these eleven steps - you'll automatically be able to pick up the guitar and start singing and playing as if you've been doing it since the day you were born.

Take each step one at a time, and practice each over and over until it becomes second nature. Then, you can move on to the next. Even if you spent a week on each step, within ten weeks you'd be playing guitar and singing at the same time.

Ok, break over, on to step 2.

Step 2

Use your imagination

Naturally, in an ideal world, you would be able to practice 24/7. But as we know, life isn't like that! There are times when you haven't got a guitar to hand, or moments where it wouldn't be appropriate to sing.

Now, Step 2 is in fact a step that should run alongside all the other remaining nine steps. So make a point of making it part of your daily habits, as you move through the other steps.

Not all time has to feel wasted

I always find it frustrating when I am somewhere where I don't really want to be, knowing that this was precious time that could be spent better, such as, oh I don't know....playing the guitar!

You could be sat at a Christening that you don't really want to be at, because you don't really know the family all that well.

Or perhaps you're sat in traffic, tearing your hair out because you're not moving anywhere.

They are frustrating situations, but you simply have to make the best of them. While your trusty guitar may not be there in your arms, there are certain things you can do to make the best of a 'bad' situation.

When you aren't physically practicing, there is still no reason why you can't be subconsciously practicing. But what do I mean by this?

Well for instance, what do you think about when you go to sleep at night? Chances are it's something that's causing you worry, or something that happened during the day? And more often than not, these thoughts keep you awake. It can often lead to a frustrating night of broken sleep, if any.

Or indeed when you are sat in traffic, or sat on a church pew that you wish you weren't perched upon....or how about when you're stood in the supermarket queue? Do you daydream about, well, nothing? How about instead of wasting this time on redundant thoughts, we try some techniques that could just make the difference to your learning...

Positive Daydreaming

The next time you are somewhere you'd rather not be, try a bit of "positive" daydreaming. For instance, when you're next in a situation like waiting in a supermarket queue, pick the song that you currently wish to learn, and simply start by imagining it playing in your head, with you performing it.

Don't allow yourself to be too distracted by your daydreaming - you need to remain aware of your surroundings! There are far better moments for when more intensive imaginings can take place - I will cover this shortly.

Back to the supermarket queue - gently tap your foot along to the music playing in your head, taking care not to freak out the old lady in front of you!

And remember to make sure you don't drift away too much as you reach the front of the queue...visualize the chords, and imagine your hand playing them – better still, form the chord shapes in your hand – discreetly of course. You can certainly do this when you're in traffic in your car, or walking somewhere.

One technique to take this a step further, is if you have a credit card handy, use this for your guitar fretting hand, by having the card in your palm, and forming the chords on the card. In addition, it's worth pressing the tips of your fingers into the side of the card when you can. This is almost the same sensation as putting your fingers on guitar strings. What this will do is firm up your fingertips, so that the next time you come to play after time away from the guitar, it won't hurt your fingertips so much. This hardening of the fingertips are known as calluses.

By repeating positive images of successfully completed tasks, we are committing them to something we call 'muscle memory'. This isn't literally a muscle, but instead refers simply to the act of repeating a task until it becomes committed to memory, to the point that it becomes automatic. This can be through physically performing a task and also imagining it.

For instance tying a tie, or tying your shoelaces - you fought with it initially as a child, but now when you need to do up your shoes, you tie your laces without even thinking about it.

The exact same thing happens with everything you are learning in this book. Whether it's a new chord you are learning, or the lyrics to a song, or, as is the aim of this book, playing guitar and singing at the same time - the more you practice and repeat an act, the more likely you are to commit it to your muscle memory i.e. that cache of information stored in your brain, containing tasks you know off by heart.

However, we do need to be careful when attempting to commit something to muscle memory. Learning a new task and committing it to muscle memory relies on your brain taking one huge assumption - that for the task you are repeating, you are doing it well. Therefore practice doesn't always make perfect.

Think about it for a minute. If you are learning the chords to a song, but are making mistakes over and over, your muscle memory can't distinguish that you're doing it wrong. Therefore if you are making mistakes over and over, you are committing these mistakes to your muscle memory, and not the correct way to play the song.

This is why I get you to record yourself throughout this book, so that you can identify the mistakes, and ensure you are adding the best bits to the data bank that is your muscle memory.

This is also the reason I get you to break down songs into chunks, so that you can become great at a small part, and then another small part, then another, until the sum of all these small parts adds up to the successful completion of the whole song.

Patience is imperative here, so it is key to repeat small parts slowly, paying attention to the recordings you make and analyzing where the mistakes might be. And iron these out. We don't want these in your muscle memory. Once mistakes are committed to muscle memory, they are very difficult to eradicate.

We are therefore training your muscle memory in two ways. Firstly, anytime that it is appropriate to do so, and your full concentration isn't currently required, visualize yourself successfully performing your song of choice, picturing your hands hitting the right chords in the right place, singing the words perfectly in time and in tune, with the crowd adulating you.

This ensures you are committing positive images to your muscle memory.

Secondly, by practicing over and over, recording yourself as you go along, you can identify (if any) the 'bad bits', and eradicate them, so as to ensure the only bits going into your muscle memory are the good bits.

If you bear this in mind throughout this book, you'll be giving yourself a great platform to build upon as you go through this learning process.

Drifting off to sleep at night

Let's take the daydreaming a step further and build out the scene in your mind. I mentioned above a better time for this, so try the following every night.

As you close your eyes, take a few long deep breaths into your diaphragm, and picture yourself somewhere where you are going to be playing guitar and singing at the same time. It might be a concert, or in front of family and friends, or just sat at home on your own. Just pick a positive scene of you playing to your audience.

Picture the scene, you with your guitar in a comfortable position, sat or stood relaxed with the correct posture. Just let your mind drift into this scenario.

Now take it a step further and imagine yourself successfully singing and playing. See your fingers making the chords on the fretboard; visualize your strumming hand playing perfectly in time. Hear the song in your head. Imagine your crowd responding positively, your family and friends smiling, singing along, or the audience cheering wildly.

This is the key – night after night, by repeatedly drumming into your head these positive images of you completing the task successfully, not making a mistake, everything perfectly in time, your "crowd" responding positively, you can begin to program your brain to the point where it can't distinguish between actually doing it and simply picturing it.

Your brain takes for granted that this is a naturally occurring image. Just because you are not literally playing the guitar and singing, but are just there lying in your bed, it doesn't mean your brain can't still "learn" to do it. Again, we are filling your muscle memory.

And while you're doing this exercise, you can do some of the deep breathing exercises we mentioned earlier to help build up your lung capacity, which will aid your singing. Multitasking!

Keep doing this every night when you go to bed, and before long it will be that ingrained in your brain that it will start to become second nature when you pick up your guitar. It's certainly worth doing this every night throughout this learning process. Put yourself in front of a different 'crowd' every night, perhaps building up to Wembley Stadium! It's actually also a good technique for getting to sleep. Every time I've imagined myself playing a gig, I only ever get through two or three songs before I've nodded off.

With the above techniques, we're programming your subconscious mind to rule your conscious mind. So whenever the opportunity arises, and it's appropriate to do so, try this technique. It's far more powerful than you might think. Just pick the song you wish to learn, and make it part of your daily/nightly routine.

Live and breathe the song at every opportunity, even in your subconscious. Instead of thinking about something you may or may not have forgotten to do at work or school, try using this thinking time more constructively - it could make all the difference to your learning.

And to recap...

- Make the most of 'wasted' moments, during the day and when drifting off to
- Imagine yourself successfully performing a song, with no mistakes
- Make this part of your everyday routine

Step 3

Memorize the words

Hopefully now the song you wish to learn is at the forefront of your mind 24/7, and you're visualizing your successful performance at every opportunity, committing it to your muscle memory.

Now we need to ensure you know the song lyrics inside out. The priority here is to absolutely memorize singing the song, off by heart.

The chances are, if it's a favorite song of yours, you already know the words. But if you don't, you need to make it your business to learn it word for word, every rise and fall of the tune.

A good test for knowing when you're ready is if you drive (or do any task that requires concentration), if you can sing along to a song without even thinking about it, then you're well on your way. i.e. multi-tasking as you sing.

So it may be that you'll need to find the lyrics online, and to print them off. This will help with learning the words. The only way you can reach your goal here is to keep practicing. If you love a song enough, you'll have no problems learning it.

Ensure you pay attention to how the lyrics fit in with the music, and where any accents are. Even if you know the song already, I would suggest printing the lyrics off anyway.

Then, as you listen back to the song, make a mark on the page where you hear the chord changes. Just write a symbol that you'll recognize above the corresponding word. Then, in future, as you read the lyrics while singing along to the song, you have a visual representation of where the chord changes are.

It's not necessary to know what the chords are at this point, just get a feel for when the chord changes occur. Just audibly accent the word a change corresponds to - for instance if the line you are singing is "You mean the world to me", and a chord change occurs on the word "world", then sing this word louder than the others. "You mean the WORLD to me". It will help to reinforce into your brain where these chord changes take place.

If you are unable to work out where the chord changes occur in a song, don't worry, sometimes it can take a little longer for some people to tune their hearing into it. It's nothing to worry about, and this won't hinder your progress in any way.

You can buy sheet music for practically any song or album that has been released, and the great thing about these is that they show you chord boxes above the places a chord change occurs. Sheet music often has the lyrics printed alongside the music, therefore giving you a visual representation of where the lyrics fit alongside the chords.

This is perfect for us, and really helps us get an idea of how the lyrics and music fit together.

Foot tapping

If you're able to multi-task at this point, then try to introduce tapping your foot along to the beat as you sing along to the song. Listen for the timing and the dominant drum beat and tap your foot in time. Many songs will allow you to tap to a count of "1,2,3,4", so listen out for a simple beat such as that, and try to ingrain the rhythm into your conscience. This is all designed to help when it comes to playing the chords to the song for the first time.

Air Guitar

And if you are comfortable throwing something else into the mix, once you've got the hang of the above, then try "air strumming" (i.e. playing an imaginary guitar) with your strumming hand, and try to identify what you think the rhythm of the guitar chords might be. Even if you can't spot this immediately, just "air strumming" along to the drum beat will help. Any kind of head-start we can give you at this point will only help later on.

Time for a recap...

- Get comfortable
- Find the lyrics to the song
- Learn them off by heart
- Accentuate the words that correspond with chord changes. Mark these on the lyric sheet
- Tap your foot, air drum or air strum at the same time

Step 4

Learning the rhythm

You've got the lyrics tattooed into your memory, you've got a feel for the sound and where you think the chord changes might occur, now it's time to switch your attention to the rhythm of the song.

What we're aiming for is that your guitar playing needs to be automatic before you can introduce anything else into the mix. So ignore the lyrics during this part of the process, for now we are concentrating on getting your guitar playing super tight.

Sit down or stand up?

First things first, when you're playing guitar, make sure that you're sat down! At least until later on, when you're more confident.

Standing up at this point just gives you something else to think about, as your back starts aching, or you start pacing around the room.

Of course, if you insist on standing up and find it more relaxing, then do so. Later on when you are further down the line, if you are planning on performing on a stage, you'll need to learn to play while standing up. You'll remember earlier in the book, I recommended that when singing you should aim to stand up with good posture.

But sitting down at this point will just give you less to think about until you get the hang of playing and singing together. Then you can progress to standing up.

Whatever you choose to do, the most important thing right now is that you are COMFORTABLE. We will introduce standing up later, as part of getting you multi-tasking on auto-pilot.

First off, we're going to pay no attention to the chords. Even if you've already sourced the sheet music for the song, put it to one side for a moment. We just want to get the hang of the strumming rhythm first.

Sing the strumming pattern

This might sound weird, but it's a really useful technique for familiarizing yourself with the rhythm of a song. It's how I break down songs when I'm learning them, and helps me to memorize the rhythm.

When I say 'sing the strumming pattern', it refers to verbally mimicking the rhythm of the guitar. For instance we might verbalize the guitar strumming to Songbird by Oasis into:

jun-jee jiggy-jiggy jun-jee jiggy-jiggy jun-jee

In my own head, this is how the guitar rhythm sounds. Hey, I could be wrong and it might sound differently to you, but if someone asked me to "sing" the rhythm to the song, I would sing it as the phrase above. It doesn't have to be a perfect replica at this stage.

The great thing is, you can sing this mimicked rhythm in your head whenever you are doing Step 2 - positive daydreaming and drifting off to sleep.

Furthermore, Songbird is about as easy as it gets with its simple rhythm and 3 chord G, D/F#, Em sequence, and therefore is a great song to start on. So if you struggled to find songs to add to your list earlier, consider making a start with this song.

If the song you're learning has a strumming pattern that is slightly harder than other songs, and you find you're having trouble getting the hang of it, don't worry. There is absolutely no reason why your version of the song has to be a carbon copy of the original.

In fact, there's more credit to you if you put your own spin on the song. So don't be afraid to make up your own rhythm if it makes the song more comfortable for you to play. It doesn't matter at this point, since we're not performing in front of anyone.

Muting the strings

Put the song on your music player, and grab your guitar. Now, at this stage we're not going to be playing the chords initially, however we don't want to just play the guitar with open strings as it will sound horrible.

So let's MUTE the strings. Just gently lay your fretting fingers across the strings, so that when you strum with your strumming hand, the strings do not ring, but instead make a percussive, click sound.

All we want to hear at this point is the sound of your plectrum hitting the strings. And this will help with getting a hang of the rhythm you've just identified. Without the distraction of the sounds of the chords, you can concentrate on your timing.

For instance, try listening to a song like "Wonderwall" where the guitar strumming is really easy to hear. Verbally mimic the strumming first. Then try strumming along to the song with the strings muted, and get some feeling into your strumming hand. Keep the motion nice and fluid and relaxed. Let there be no tension.

Remember, forget about the chords for this part of the process, and just get a hang of the strumming.

If you want to and feel able to, you can try humming along to the tune of the song over this muted strumming.

Feeling a bit more confident? If you're satisfied you've got the hang of the muted rhythm at this point, try distracting yourself by strapping your guitar around your neck and strum while walking around, or watching television. If you're strumming continues successfully even with something else taking your attention, then congratulations, you are starting to use your subconscious for your guitar playing!

Your recap for this step:

- Mimic and verbalize the rhythm
- Mute the strings and play the rhythm
- Distract yourself while strumming

Step 5

Learning the chords

Which chords are used?

Now switch off your music player, as this will only serve as a distraction initially. Grab your chord sheet for the song you want to learn, and if it's not already in your hands, pick up your guitar again.

First off, scan your eyes over the chord sheet, and see which chords are used. Most sheet music lists all the chords used in a song, at the top of the very first page. If you've followed the song selection process outlined in step 1, then you should have in front of you a song with all open chords.

Firstly, just strum through all the chords used, in the order they appear at the top of the chord sheet, just so you get used to moving between them. You're not playing the song at this point, just randomly playing the chords that feature.

Play each chord for a count of 8, then change to the next chord. Start off with just down strokes in a constant counting rhythm, then once you've got the hang of that, change the strumming to down-up strokes, still counting to 8 for each chord.

With learning the chords, the part you most need to take notice of is what the strumming hand is doing. The chords shouldn't even be part of your conscious mind, these should be automatic - almost as though your left hand has a mind of its own.

Just switch off your mind and aim to get your fretting hand moving between the chords automatically. You can work on this even more if you have a friend or family member that is willing to help.

Start playing the first chord of the song, in a constant down-up rhythm, and ask your assistant to call out at random intervals chord names that feature in the song. When they have called the next chord name, your fretting hand needs to change to form this chord, while your strumming hand keeps playing the same rhythm. There must be no break in this strumming. This exercise helps you get used to chord changes, and gets you to maintain a solid strumming rhythm.

The chord changes

You're now going to listen to the song again on your music player, and look at where the chord changes are on the chord sheet. What I want you to do now, is listen to the whole song, and strum each chord ONCE on each chord change, ensuring you play the chords in the order they appear in the song.

Try this technique until you get an understanding of where the chord changes take place in relation to the lyrics. Let your eyes follow the lyrics as you strum each chord.

Keep going with this until you're comfortable, then put the song back to the beginning again and add in an extra strum in between each chord change, so that you're playing each chord twice. For instance, if you were playing G, C and D in a repeating progression to a count of 4, it would have counted out as :

G   C   D

1 2 3 4 1 2 3 4 1 2 3 4

But with the additional strums, we're now playing:

G G C C D D

1 2 3 4 1 2 3 4 1 2 3 4

And when you've got the hang of this, progress to playing a chord on every beat i.e. On 1,2,3,4.

Learning your song

If you've already cracked the song, feel free to skip this part.

Rather than jumping in and trying to play the whole song, we're going to break it down into intro, verse, chorus, middle eight (if there is one), outro and take each one individually. We can piece them all together later.

You want to learn one part of the song until you've got it to a good standard whereby you are able to do it without thinking. Then, you can move on to the next part.

The way to do this is by turning the song on its head. We'll explain why in a moment, but what we will do is start with one part of the song, and keep adding another bit until you are playing the whole song. At this point, it's just you and your guitar, no background music.

First off, you learn the outro of the song, then next time around you play the final chorus and the outro, then the next time it's the final verse, final chorus and outro etc etc. Just keep tagging on the next piece of the song until you've reached adding the intro as the final piece. This way, on your final run through, you will be playing the WHOLE song for the first time!

The temptation normally, is to start learning a song from the start. The problem with this is, unless you play the song right the way through every time, there are parts near the end of the song that you aren't practicing as often. Starting at the end ensures you are more familiar with the whole song, rather than just the parts near the beginning. Besides, it forces you to think more, when you break up the song into an unfamiliar format.

So recall your mimicked rhythm from earlier and start strumming the outro to the song. This time, you won't be muting the strings.

As you're not listening to the song, you can even slow it down to a tempo that is comfortable for you. If you want to hum along as you play, ignore the fact that it might sound a little strange at this tempo - but who cares, you're the only one in the room! If you need to listen to the actual song for reference at any point, feel free to do so. And keep recalling your mimicked rhythm to keep your strumming in check.

Once you've perfected the outro, move on to playing the final chorus and the outro. A typical song would require you playing the song in the following way:

1. Outro
2. Final chorus, outro
3. Middle eight, final chorus, outro
4. Second chorus, middle eight, final chorus, outro
5. Second verse, second chorus, middle eight, final chorus, outro
6. First chorus, second verse, second chorus, middle eight, final chorus, outro
7. First verse, first chorus, second verse, second chorus, middle eight, final chorus, outro
8. Intro, first verse, first chorus, second verse, second chorus, middle eight, final chorus, outro

Just remember at this point the "3 p's". Practice, practice, practice. The more you can repeat any process, the more it becomes a habit.

If you can get your playing to become habit, then you've already covered off part of the overall exercise, giving you less to concentrate on.

If you are still playing the song at a slower tempo, slowly build up the tempo with each time you play the song, until it matches that of the real song itself.

Multi-tasking

Once you're able to strum the song right the way through, I want you to play the whole song from the beginning, and once again try a bit of multi-tasking at the same time, such as walking around (make sure you still have a guitar strap attached to your guitar!). Then progress on to watching television while playing.

Carry on playing the guitar, but at the same time concentrate 100% on what is on the television. Watch it as you would normally, and switch off your mind from what you are doing on the guitar. The more you can engross yourself in the television the better. We need to get you playing without even realizing.

This will help enormously when you come to sing over the top, as both activities are essentially multi-tasking.

We want to get this chord playing automatic, then you can progress to complicated tasks like reading a newspaper or a book, or having a conversation with someone. You've got to separate what you are thinking from what you are doing, to the point of auto-pilot.

See if you can recite back part of what you've just read from the newspaper or give a brief overview of what you just watched on the television, or recall the conversation you just had.

If you are able to do this, it will show that you were concentrating more on what your eyes and ears were taking in than on your actual playing.

This is what we want to be happening, so well done! You're finally splitting your conscious and subconscious.

Now for a bit of fun - put the song on your music player and play along to it in full. Congratulations, you're now part of the band!

A recap...

- Single strum the chord on each chord change
- Add in another strum in between each chord change, then each beat
- Play the song in reverse, starting with the outro
- Strum the song while walking around
- Play to the song in full

Step 6

Record your rhythm, sing over it

Now we're going to start putting together your very first recording of you playing and singing the song. But not at the same time, at least not just yet...

If you have a metronome, then set it to coincide with the beat of the song, or choose your own speed to suit your playing. If you've not used one before, a metronome is simply a device to help keep your playing in time. It plays a click at identical intervals, which you can set. The more frequent the clicks, the faster the tempo.

If you don't own a metronome, then if you've got a Smartphone like an iPhone or Android phone, you can easily download an app – just search the app store on your phone.

Now put the song on and feel the beat of it, counting along, then set your metronome playing and speed it up and slow it down until it matches the tempo of the song. Alternatively, your chord sheet may show the tempo of the song. If so, you should be able to enter this number into your metronome, and instantly have the correct tempo. Of course, you can always slow down the tempo to something more manageable for your first few tries. Whatever feels most comfortable.

Now turn the song off

Once you've got the metronome set up, all you need to do now is play along with it. Don't worry about the singing for now, just get your strumming in time with the click track.

Once again, start off just playing each chord once on the chord change, then build up to introduce more frequent strumming. Once you are comfortable, you can try playing the mimicked rhythm you came up with earlier, until finally, you are playing the whole song, in time with the metronome.

Record your playing

Once you're comfortable with this and think you've got the hang of it, it's time to record yourself playing.

Find yourself a recording device - most mobile phones have a recording function, but if you're already using your phone for the metronome, then you might need to kindly ask to borrow someone else's phone! Or record on your PC/Mac. Alternatively, you could go super "old-skool", and find a tape recorder or dictaphone.

Now record yourself playing along to the metronome. Don't be frightened of this, it's going to help you heaps. This is useful for two reasons:

You will get an idea of how far you've come already when you play it back, and...

You will use this as a backing track which you are going to sing the song over.

A far more elegant way of doing this is to use a piece of software like Garageband, which you can download on an iPhone/iPad or iMac. You can then record individual "tracks" into this, which then negates the need for two phones! It also has a built in metronome. If you get stuck, there are a wealth of help videos on YouTube which show you how to use Garageband.

If you're not quite ready to strum the chords unaccompanied, and would still prefer the guidance of the song, then don't worry. If you've got some earphones, you can listen to the song, and still record yourself strumming the chords. Just leave out the metronome for now. Sooner or later you will get to the point where you can do this without hearing the music.

Just take this at a pace that is comfortable for you, and don't put pressure on yourself. You WILL get the hang of this with practice. If you're only comfortable playing the one chord strums, then record this. If you are able to play the mimicked rhythm, then great, record this over the metronome.

Sing over the recording

Once you've got your recording, it's time to sing along to it. Don't worry about what your guitar playing sounds like at this point – we just want you to match up what you were playing with the singing.

As you sing along to your recording, listen to the rhythm of the chords you played and hear where they fit in with the lyrics. Tap your foot or beat out the rhythm on your thighs to engross yourself in the rhythm.

And if you're sat there with a second mobile phone/recording device, then if you really want to, you could record yourself singing along to your backing track. (You'll be able to use the phone that had the metronome, as we don't need the metronome for this part).

Play this second recording back and you'll begin to get an idea of how it all fits together. You can be proud of yourself – what you are playing back is YOU singing and playing guitar. You're now well on your way to doing both at the same time...

And your recap...

- Set your metronome to the tempo of the song
- Play along until you are able to play the whole song
- Record yourself
- Sing over the recording, and record this if you wish

Now you know what's coming up next don't you...

Step 7

Record your singing, play over it

Yes, we're reversing the roles now.

Now I want you to start recording again, playing the metronome, at the same speed you have already set up, but this time sing over it. We don't want any guitar playing at this point, just you signing the song over a metronome. This will work wonders for your timing. Trust me.

Now don't be shy - you may not like your singing voice, particularly unaccompanied - but if you're hoping to perform in the future, then you're going to need to overcome these fears. Besides, you'll be playing this back to yourself in a bit, so you better get used to it!

Chances are, you won't sing in key, so if it helps (and you are able to), then listen to your guitar recording on your earphones, and sing along to that. Or, if you're using a programme like Garageband for your recording, you can always auto-tune, if that's your bag.

Play over the recording

Once you've got a recording of you singing over the click track, that you're happy with (or at the very least, fairly happy with), then it's time to play it back, and play along with it on your guitar.

Again, listen out for where the rhythm, chord changes and accents fit in with the lyrics. We're engraving the song into your memory now - we've dissected, sliced and diced it, turned it inside out and are now heading towards piecing it all together again.

Once again, if you are in a position to, you can record yourself playing guitar over your singing backing track. Then play this back and hear what it sounds like. Which recording of the two is the best? Was it you playing along to your singing, or you singing along to your playing? Which did you find easier?

Whichever way you found easiest, you can be pleased that you have achieved these two steps, because you really are motoring – so give yourself a pat on the back. We're going to be moving this on now...

A little recap...

- Sing over the metronome, with the same tempo
- Record yourself
- Play along to the recording
- Record yourself if you wish
- Compare your two recordings

Ready for step 8?

Step 8

Humming and "La-La'ing" while playing

Now it's back to the original song itself, leaving your backing track to one side.

Now that you've got the hang of playing the chords, and have a sound grip of the rhythm and chord changes, and a good idea of where the lyrics fit in, it's time to start introducing the melody over the top of you playing the chords, AT THE SAME TIME.

Hum along

So, before you start singing along to the track (the actual song, not your recording from the last step), we're going to get you first humming along as you play the chords. It doesn't have to be particularly loud or tuneful, just gently hum along the tune as you strum the chords.

You can start playing the chords by just strumming a single chord on each chord change, then progress to playing the full rhythm, using your mimicked rhythm again. Whatever you're comfortable with.

Remember, if you followed the earlier chapter on singing, humming is a great way to warm up your vocal chords, so all the time you are doing this, you are doing some good.

It's up to you whether you are doing this with the song playing or not, but it might help to do it without, to force your subconscious to recall the melody without any assistance.

La la along

Then, when you feel ready to move on, you can progress to la-la-la'ing along instead. This is a bit more involved than humming as it requires paying more attention to the tune, and is the next step towards singing and playing for the first time.

Again, don't worry about the quality of your singing at this point, or if you mess up. IT DOESN'T MATTER. Practice makes perfect.

You don't even need to "la-la" in tune, just randomly la-la any old tune. The key here is to get you separating out what you are playing from what you are "singing".

The fact you're not having to concentrate on singing a particular tune is a step towards singing it properly.

Once your brain has made the distinction between the la-la'ing being separate from the guitar playing, you can ramp it up further by la-la'ing in tune.

Now, we're not concerned about the rhythm while we do this, we're just introducing the ability to sing while thinking about where the chords sit alongside the lyrics.

As I said, feel free to do this exercise with the 'one strum on each chord change' technique. Once you've got these two things joined up, you can think about introducing the rhythm.

As with all exercises in this book, make sure you're ready first — there's no point rushing yourself at this stage, not when you are so close to your goal.

Recap time...

- Play the rhythm slowly, hum the melody
- Then progress to "la la" the melody

Step 9

Speak the words while playing

Now that you've managed to hum the song and play the chords, and you've been able to la-la the song as you play the chords, it's time to ramp it up further by SPEAKING the words as you play.

By throwing the words into the mix, it gives your brain a little more to think about....which is why I stressed the importance of knowing the song inside out first, so that you don't have to THINK about it.

Just consider for a minute your most favorite songs in the world – you just sing these without even thinking about the words don't you? Well hopefully this is the case with whatever song you are learning here.

Take this exercise at a speed comfortable for you, and don't worry too much about speaking in tune. We're just trying to get you matching the lyrics to their correct position alongside the chords.

Believe me, it won't sound rubbish. There are some classic songs that have been sung in a spoken tone.

For instance Mmm Mmm Mmm Mmm by Crash Test Dummies is one, and many Leonard Cohen tracks, such as the magical track Suzanne. And Cohen is rightly regarded by many, many people as a musical genius, so you are currently in good company by speaking your song.

You never know, you may have stumbled on a singing style perfect for you – it could become your trademark!

As you strum each chord, accentuate the word from the lyrics that you are strumming on. This again helps ingrain the song into your head. You don't have to actually 'sing' at this point, just speak the lyrics as you play your single chord strums.

Once you've got the hang of these single strums, add in another strum so that you are strumming down-up, down-up.

Then, as we have mentioned throughout, play your "verbalized" rhythm of the song. Once you've got this playing cleanly, clearly and in time, introduce the talking of the lyrics over the top.

If it helps, you can always record this, to see how it sounds, and to spot any anomalies with the words and the chords. If you spot any part where you've lost your timing slightly, you can hone in on this and seek to correct it.

If you can face listening back to yourself, then playing and recording, then analyzing and correcting, over and over, it is going to help you immeasurably.

Your recap...

- Play the rhythm slowly, speak the words, accentuate words that correspond with chord changes

Step 10
Putting it all together

Before we get you playing and singing the song unaccompanied, you need to make sure you're comfortable with performing along to the song first. Only then can you think about "going it alone" unaccompanied.

So start by playing along to the song, until your strumming becomes automatic. A good idea is to put the song on "repeat" on your music player, so that you have no interruptions. Feel your strumming melt into the music, and find your mind disassociate from your hand. Then, try to introduce some singing over the top, in time with the singer on the song.

If you are able to, it really is worth spending as long as possible on each step, but of course, we are all the same in that we just want to get on with it and start singing and playing. I can't really blame you, I was exactly the same. But in time, I knew the only way I was going to get there was through patience and practice.

Are you sure that you have spent long enough on the previous steps? Were there any that you had trouble with?

When you feel ready to try singing and playing without the song playing, it's certainly worth playing the song slowly first, before you build up to the correct tempo of the song. Eventually you'll get to a good speed that just flows naturally. Work through the single chord strums technique, then double strums, then build up to your mimicked rhythm.

You have got to switch your mind off from what you are doing. This means, DO NOT think about the chords you are playing, DO NOT think about where your fingers are going on the fretboard.

The aforementioned needs to be taken care of by your subconscious, which is why you need to ABSOLUTELY know the songs' chords and lyrics off by heart. The reason for this is because your conscious mind will be concentrating on the singing. If you have followed the previous steps, you will already have achieved this.

We then need to ensure you are matching up the timing of the singing with the chords you are playing. You can't allow either part to get ahead or behind the other - they need to work in tandem.

Just remember that, if you have a good steady rhythm being played on your guitar, then this becomes the backbone of what you're doing. It is the singing that melds itself around the chords.

The singing must keep in time with the guitar. If you allow your guitar playing to mould to the singing, then chances are you will find your rhythm going out of time.

When you've attempted to play a song, you may have found that your strumming inadvertently falls in tandem with your singing, whereby you strum once for each syllable. This is common, and simply your brain being unable to separate the two tasks. Don't worry, this will come in time.

This probably sounds scary stuff, but you have come so far that you really shouldn't be put off easily any more.

Chances are there are some songs you like that have fairly complicated rhythms and pretty tricky singing. This is why we have picked songs to begin with where the rhythm of the guitar is almost in tandem with the singing. By this we mean each strum of your guitar almost has a single word associated to it.

A good example of this is Wish You Were Here by Pink Floyd - have a listen to the song and you'll hear what I mean. You can find how to play this and other songs over on the Facebook Group.

With songs like this, both the singing and the rhythm are supporting each other, and prevent you losing time on either front. These are great tunes to start out with, and will aid you in moving on to songs with slightly more complex structures.

When you try it out for the first time, if you find yourself going out of time, or your rhythm is becoming a little stilted, ignore it and plough onwards. You've got to ignore the mistakes while you are learning, and just carry on.

You'll look back fondly on the times you couldn't do it. Just start slowly, and build up the tempo as it becomes more comfortable.

Do it in the dark

As you get the hang of it, a great technique to try is playing the song in the dark, or just to shut your eyes. This forces you to concentrate on the sound you are making, and disassociates you from your surroundings, and strangely, gives you a feeling of control in what you are doing.

If playing in the dark isn't an option for you, then you can basically just play without looking at the fretboard. This dissociates your brain from what your fingers are doing.

Recap...

- Ensure you're ready
- Play slowly, starting with single strums on chord changes, and sing
- Progress to playing in the dark

Step 11
Playing to an audience for the first time

Now it's time to pick your audience. You've been visualizing in your head what this might be like, now it's time to do it for real.

You're bound to be a bit nervous at this point. There aren't many people that don't get nervous about singing in front of an audience, so don't panic. Even Robbie Williams has admitted to suffering with stage fright, and yet he manages to cover this up with extreme confidence and bravado. I'm not suggesting you go to these lengths, but hey, it works for him. People would never know that underneath there is a bag of nerves.

If you're not quite ready for a human audience, how about something a bit fluffier...bear with me on this...

Do you have any pets, which are fairly obedient? They won't answer back for starters, so if it's criticism you fear then you'll be ok. As long as they don't start scratching the door to get out or start whimpering.

Not got pets? Find some cuddly toys or print off some face masks instead, and line them up in front of you! I know it sounds silly, but think about it, these are going to be the easiest crowds you'll ever play to, so lose yourself in the moment and pretend this is the real thing. You could even print off some photos of faces!

Make eye contact with your 'crowd', and remember to smile occasionally. You should make a point of doing this to any audience you perform to. It will make them warm to you, and their warmth radiating back to you will make it so much easier and more pleasant for you, like a tiny confidence booster. When you're laying your soul bare on a stage, any kind of ego boost is very welcome. I've played to many crowds where I don't feel like I'm getting anything back, but you have to learn to not be bothered by it. Just keep on rocking!

Worried about "looking silly"? You've got to push these ideas from your mind – how many performers do you know where you've thought, "they look silly" as they are baring their soul on stage with their voice and guitar. Exactly.

Try this. Put yourself in front of a mirror and pull the most ridiculous face you can think of. Have a little laugh at how strange you look, and bear in mind that anything you do on stage is not going to look anywhere as bad as the face you just pulled!

Seriously, you don't need to spend wasted energy worrying about how you're going to look. If you start worrying, it's only going to affect your performance.

The one thing you want to ensure is that you are giving an honest performance, and if you aren't, your subjects are going to pick up on it. So shut out any preconceived ideas you have, and focus on the MUSIC. That is what we're all here for after all, isn't it?

The real thing - performance

Ok, you've reached the very final stage of this process. The cuddly toys are packed away. Now it's time for your first live performance in front of a human being.

Choose your subject wisely. You want them to be receptive and supportive, but you also need them to not be afraid of being critical (constructively). And you also need to be able to accept criticism gracefully, and use it positively. You are still on this journey, and not at the destination. So let all feedback, good and bad, make you a better performer.

Performing on stage to a crowd? Just accept that you are going to feel nervous, and embrace it. It will make you put in a better performance. And believe me, once you've got past the first couple of lines of the first song, the nerves will gradually fade as the crowd gets warmed up. Stand or sit with confidence, remembering to focus on your posture.

Remember the audience is there to see YOU, so take confidence from that. Do not see the audience as something to be frightened of – they are just a mass of individual people.

If you can single out some smiling faces, then focus on them if it helps. Or if you'd rather not look people in the eye, then focus on the area above the audience's heads.

Perhaps it's a bar at the back, or a burger van — whatever it is, focus on it — but not too much, you don't want your audience to think you're not "with them", and your mind is somewhere else!

Don't forget, the crowd is WITH you, not AGAINST you. Ignore them, and you may lose them. So...

...if you don't mind a bit of banter, you can talk to your audience. Talk to them like you would to one person, as this helps make the crowd before you feel smaller.

A great example of someone who engages brilliantly with his audience is Liam Gallagher — his cheeky, comical asides will inevitably give him a boost when his audience laughs back with him (not at him!)

Worried about messing up? Believe it or not, people love it when an artist messes up. It shows that they are only human. The key is not to turn it into a melt-down, but plough onwards, not allowing any kind of degradation in the remainder of your performance. Just pretend like it never happened. Ideally, don't even mention it. If it makes you feel better, you can apologize at the end of the song, but leave it at that and move on.

Besides, any kind of error could end up going viral on YouTube! Many people believe that there is no such thing as bad publicity, so don't even worry about it. Just roll with it.

Bear in mind all of the above, and you will be greeted by a warm applause at the end of your performance. YOU are in control of that room, no one else. The microphone is in your power, not theirs. Anything they can say, you can say a hell of a lot louder!

Optional: Taking things a step further

This section may not apply to everyone, but the likelihood is there will be some songwriters amongst you.

We mentioned at the very start of this book those people that audition on television talent shows, especially when they are singing and performing their own songs. For starters it is an incredibly brave thing to do, when you consider the audience of millions they are getting on a Saturday night.

Ordinarily, the temptation would be to sing a well-known song that everyone knows. It ensures the crowd gets on your side as they sing along with the chorus. But this often isn't the most sure-fire way of being noticed.

Firstly, you will need to do a good job of it. As you are singing a song that is in the national conscience, they will have a preconceived idea of how it SHOULD sound. So if you plough in there and murder a classic, you're on very dangerous ground!

Therefore an alternative is to put your own unique take on the song, and make it stand out from the original, but for the right reasons. However, this is still dangerous ground, and more risky than just singing a carbon copy of the original. You'll need to have real confidence in your version of the song.

Another option then is to sing your own song that you have written. One advantage is you get to dictate the rhythm and melody, and make it as simple to play as you like. And you have an opportunity to make your performance more "believable", as the song came from you. Furthermore, nobody will have ever heard the song before, so can't comment on whether it sounds like the original. It IS the original! But this also means they won't be able to sing along with it. Unless it is instantly catchy and memorable. More on that in a moment.

Singing and playing a song you have written means you will have to be prepared for an eerie silence until the end of the song, as the audience sits listening, not able to sing along. This silence will hopefully be only broken when you reach the end of the song and the audience gives you a rapturous applause and standing ovation.

But how do we ensure this kind of reception to songs we've written?

Write from the heart

The most important thing with your song is that it has to be BELIEVABLE. If the audience sense that any part of your performance isn't genuine and from the heart, you're in danger of them turning on you.

So when you write your songs, aim to write from personal experience. Don't make yourself sound like you are above everyone else, but ensure there is a human touch to everything you write. If your song is about something personal to you, it will make it far easier for you to inject emotion into your performance.

Sing from the heart

Every single performance you make simply HAS to be the best you can possibly give. At the same time, if you can guarantee to yourself that you will seek to improve on the previous performance, you've got the makings of a professional musician.

If what you are singing about resonates with your audience, then you've done your job. They don't even need to have an affinity with what you are singing about - as long as it is believable and honest, they will be putty in your hands.

Rhyming

We are taught at school about rhyming and how it is the core element that drives poetry and music. Yet in truth, there is a great deal of fine poetry written with no rhyming structure whatsoever. The same can be said of songs. Many, many songs are written with little or no rhyme.

What this means for you is that you mustn't feel restricted to making your song rhyme. Of course, it offers a nice structure and is easy on the ear, but the desire to rhyme the word at the end of each sentence are shackles you don't want to impose on yourself right now. Just let the words flow.

Chords

The lyrics and melody to your song must be in tandem with each other. We won't go into the mechanics of notes and why they fit with certain chords; there are countless books already available on the subject.

Choosing the chords for your song needn't be a chore. One simple solution is to take what already works.

Now let me start by saying that I'm not suggesting plagiarism - far from it - but examine a handful of songs, and the chances are that some of them have identical chord structures. Mind you, statistically this would always be likely given that all music is founded on the notes A to G!

Aim to make your chord structures as unique as you can, but if you can't, simply ensuring the melody is completely original is good enough. So what chord structures could you start with?

Well, there are countless songs that use a simple G, C, D structure, repeated over and over, as is the structure G, Em, C, D frequently used. Then of course there is the most common chord sequence in history, on which rock 'n' roll as we know it is based upon - A, D, E. This is proof that it doesn't matter how simple the chord progression is.

Making it catchy

If you want a sure-fire way of capturing your audience's attention, give them a catchy little number, with an instantly catchy chorus to sing along to. Just look at any Lennon and McCartney song and you'll see what a winning formula this was for them.

The most memorable songs are those that you can sing along to the chorus having only heard it once. Think 'She Loves You' by The Beatles and there's a fine example of one of the simplest choruses in history, which at the same time makes it instantly unforgettable.

To make something 'catchy', a repeated short musical phrase can stick in the mind. Just think of the 'She Loves You' chorus. But just be sure not to overdo it.

You need to leave the audience wanting more, eagerly anticipating the chorus next time it comes around.

A chorus can often consist of the same short phrase repeated 3 times, finishing on the 4th line with a slightly different phrase. Try this structure yourself, and see how catchy you can make your chorus.

A chorus will usually appear about three times throughout a song. This is enough not to overkill the chorus, but few enough to leave the audience wanting more. Think of the chorus of a song as an old friend, that when you hear it once, you can't wait until the next time you hear it again.

What comes first? The music or lyrics?

There are no set rules with which order you are supposed to write a song. It is entirely down to preference. There are musicians that would argue for coming up with a chord sequence first, then coming up with the melody to fit over them, just as there are musicians that would argue for the opposite.

Writing the chord sequence first can sometimes 'restrict' the melody to having to fit around those chords. Whereas if you are writing the melody first, there is nothing to stop the melody taking off in all directions. In a sense you are putting up the walls of the house before setting the foundations first.

However, for the novice musician, it can be hard to know what chords are meant to fit with the melody, which is why many musicians come up with the chords first.

The best thing you can do is try both ways and see what suits you. If you've got a chord sequence written, then start by humming a tune over the top.

If you've got some words written, then the tone of the language might help you shape the melody. For instance if they are melancholy lyrics, this might be reflected in the tune, just as it would if you had more upbeat lyrics. The best thing you can do is practice over and over, refining your work to perfection.

The more you try, the more likely it is that you stumble upon a masterpiece. You could have a future Number One hit on your hands...

So where now?

Let me make this point - just because you've reached the end of this book, it doesn't mean you're now out there on your own. You've taken a plunge by following this course, and I'm not about to withdraw the life raft just yet. At least not until you're on stage at Wembley!

Still struggling with a song you want to learn?

If at any point you find you are struggling with a song, and could do with some visual clues, then there is no better guide than watching someone who already knows how to play the song.

One of the easiest ways is to simply search for the song on YouTube and find the artist performing an acoustic rendition of the song (assuming they are an artist that plays guitar). Otherwise you may have to find someone doing a cover of it. These can often be bad imitations of the real thing, so be wary of putting too much faith in their rendition.

However, this can often show to you that perhaps you're not as far off achieving your goal as you thought. If they can do it, then so can you!

Need more advice or support?

If having read this book, you'd like support from fellow musicians who've read the book, then you can visit the "How to sing and play guitar at the same time" Facebook group. This is a place to share ideas, discuss your own learning techniques, and generally help each other through the process. Why not drop by and say hi! Head to:

www.facebook.com/groups/playguitarsing.

A final recap...

Step 1: Preparation - choosing your songs

Step 2: Use your imagination

Step 3: Memorize the words

Step 4: Learning the rhythm

Step 5: Learning the chords

Step 6: Record your rhythm. Sing over it.

Step 7: Record your singing. Play over it.

Step 8: Humming and "La-la'ing" the words while playing

Step 9: Speak the words while playing

Step 10: Putting it all together

Step 11: Playing to an audience for the first time

We've only just begun...

Well that's it, you've reached the end of this book! Now the rest is up to you...

Hopefully you are now making your practicing a part of your daily routine. Who knows, maybe you've already performed your first song to an audience? Perhaps you're awaiting your talent show audition? Whatever your goal, hopefully this book has helped you towards achieving it.

If you find you are still having a few issues with getting the hang of it, just go back through the stages again and keep repeating until it becomes natural. Trust me, it will come in time. For some people it's instant, for others it takes a little longer.

Don't forget to join us over on our Facebook group, where you can learn more tips and techniques to help you along your journey.

Head to www.facebook.com/groups/playguitarsing, and say hi! You'll also find a selection of songs there that I have picked and broken down to help get you started. These are songs with simple chord progressions and easy to follow rhythms.

Finally, if you like this book, then please review it on Amazon! **Thank you and have fun!**

Bonus Chapter

To help you on your journey, I thought I would take you through the learnings of a young beginner musician by the name of Mart, who was my guinea pig when I put this book together. A nervous chap who had no confidence in his guitar playing ability, Mart was the perfect subject to be put through the 11 step formula.

You will see the steps Mart went through, the parts he found difficult and the parts he found a breeze. With any luck, Mart's experiences will help allay any fears you may have as a result of your journey. You will see as you read through the steps Mart took, that he most likely experienced the exact same things you will have!

Step 1: Preparation - choosing your songs

Being something of a heavy metal fan, Mart was already at a disadvantage in that a lot of heavy metal music can be fairly complex in it's chord arrangements and tunings. Therefore, I had to break it to him gently that we wouldn't be attempting any 'Iron Maiden' or 'Megadeth' just yet!

I asked Mart to take some time to think of songs that he liked, that had the key ingredients of consisting of only basic open chords and a simple rhythm that almost mimicked the vocal. Sadly for him, this meant a brief foray into the joys of soft rock...

After some deliberation, we settled on some simple songs, having identified the chords to the songs from some guitar tablature sites. Our shortlist consisted of:

1) Poison - Every Rose Has Its Thorn

2) Patience - Guns 'n Roses

3) The Eagles - Take It Easy

Step 2: Use your imagination

So now that Mart had his shortlist of 'easy to play' songs, his next task was to commit them to memory. First off, I asked him to print off the chords and lyrics, and get a feel for the chords involved. At this stage, I didn't want him to pick up the guitar, but instead, I wanted him to spend time thinking about the chords, and visualizing himself playing them.

Therefore for the next few days, Mart's pre-sleep ritual was imagining himself successfully playing the song, while visualizing himself correctly hitting the chords, and singing along in time. He also found he was able to take the odd minute during his working day, to daydream about playing the chords. Of course, this was always done in his own time.... (i.e. tea breaks, lunch hours)!

Step 3: Memorise the words

Mart said he quite enjoyed positive daydreaming about playing the songs, and that it was actually more rewarding than he thought it would be. I noticed that he did actually have a little bit more confidence about him that suggested he believed he was going to achieve his goals. And we hadn't even tried playing the song yet!

I asked Mart to continue to make positive daydreaming part of his daily routine, but now to ensure that he knew the words 'off by heart' to the songs we were going to learn.

He actually already knew the words to the Poison and Guns 'n Roses songs, which left him just The Eagles to get to grips with.

While he was learning the words, he made a point of making a mental note of where the chord changes took place as he sang along to the songs. Mart found that the songs he had chosen had quite defined chord changes, which were therefore easy to spot.

Mart printed off the lyrics to the songs, and made some notes on the sheets as to where the chord changes came in. He found this helped when listening to the song. As I had suggested to him, he got into the habit of nodding when a chord change came, and also tapping along with his foot or hand to get him in tune with the rhythm of the track. After four days, it was so far so good. But Mart was now itching to get started on his guitar.

He'd been patient so far, so it was only fair that he was let loose on playing the rhythm...

Step 4: Learning the rhythm

With his trusty acoustic guitar in hand, Mart set about learning the rhythm. While listening to the tracks, he muted the strings on his guitar, and strummed along in time to the guitar rhythm, while not fingering the chords at this point.

Such is the acoustic nature of the songs he'd chosen, Mart found it fairly easy to pick out the rhythm. For two days he played this muted rhythm over and over, and by the end of the second day, he had the hang of the rhythm for all three songs.

While I usually recommend learning one song at a time, Mart felt comfortable learning all three at once. If you are happy to do this, then by all means carry on. It all adds to your learning.

Step 5: Learning the chords

Mart had the rhythm well and truly learnt, so now it was time to lift his muting hand, and start playing the chords to the songs, using the same rhythm.

It took Mart a little while to get his coordination between changing chords and maintaining the constant, driving rhythms of the songs. I said to him, that any time it feels too much, simply go back to muting the strings and get the hang of the rhythm once again.

There was one particular chord change that Mart struggled with in the Guns 'n Roses song. I watched what he was doing, and saw that the chords were correct that he was playing, but there was some hesitation in his play. I noticed that his gaze was so transfixed on what his chord fretting hand was doing, that he was almost over-concentrating on it. He was able to fret the chords without any problems, therefore I felt that he needed to dissengage himself from what he was doing. So I asked him to try playing the same piece, but with his eyes shut.

He looked at me bemused at first, but was willing to try anything, as I could see he was getting a little frustrated with himself.

Much to his amazement, after 15 minutes of playing with his eyes closed, the tricky chord change came to him. By cutting himself off from what was going on in front of him, Mart was able to overcome the hesitation that was blighting his playing.

Step 6: Record your rhythm. Sing over it.

So now that Mart had the basic rhythm of the song learnt, it was time to record his playing. He had an iPhone, therefore was already in a position to record his playing with the native recording app.

When it came to playing back what he had recorded, Mart was surprised at how far he had come. "It doesn't sound too bad actually" were his words. And when he played his rendition of 'Patience' back to me, I too was impressed.

I now asked him to spend the next day or two singing over the backing track he had recorded, and listening to where the words fit the rhythm. Normally at this point I recommend that you record yourself singing over your backing track, however Mart didn't have a second recording device, so had to skip this. However I find that it is incredibly useful to be able to play back to yourself your singing over your playing. It's a rewarding moment, and helps you begin to see that your performing is starting to take shape.

Step 7: Record your singing. Play over it.

Two days later, Mart was back and raring to go. He was satisfied that he'd got his timing right, after a few attempts. By singing over the backing track he'd created, he found that he could easily pinpoint where his rhythm playing slipped out of time, as the words didn't match the rhythm. Therefore, Mart would simply re-record his rhythm playing until he was satisfied with it.

Next I asked Mart to sing along to a metronome/click-track with no musical accompaniment. At first he struggled to get the timing of the song right without being able to hear the song. Therefore, he played the song on his headphones, and sang along to it while recording on his iPhone. This therefore created another backing track of Mart singing acapella, but this time was to be used to play guitar over.

As Mart had sung along to the actual song, he knew that his singing represented the correct timing of the song. This therefore meant that he had a strong template to match his playing to.

After several run-throughs, Mart said that he felt his rhythm playing had really tightened up, as the correct timing of his singing forced his rhythm playing to fall in line.

One other piece of feedback, which EVERYONE seems to say - he hated hearing himself sing! Well, I reminded him he needed to get over this if he was planning on performing to people, and that we are often our own harshest critic. After a few plays, you will begin to get used to the sound of your own voice. And eventually, he did!

Step 8: Humming and "La-la'ing" the words while playing

Mart was beginning to feel more and more confident by the day, which was great to see. But now was to come the hardest step so far - piecing together the playing with some kind of tune over the top. The first part of this was humming the tune over his playing.

Mart struggled at first and found his playing become out of sync, due to overly concentrating on the tune. This is something that can often happen, and is perfectly normal - often you find the more you concentrate on one part, the more the other part suffers.

Once again, we returned Mart to closing his eyes while playing and humming along. With each run through, there were improvements made, until eventually, he managed to hold the tune, and keep the momentum of the rhythm. Success! Throughout this process, it really is a case of practice making perfect.

The next stage was to 'la-la' along to the rhythm, as this is halfway between humming and actually singing the words. Again, Mart chose to close his eyes while doing this.

He also later told me that he'd recorded this step, as it helped him to play it back to himself, identify any problem areas, and pick out the bits that needed attention.

Step 9: Speak the words while playing

Mart was starting to get into the habit of closing his eyes when he played his songs, which I wanted to ensure he didn't make a permanent habit. When it comes to performing on stage, most audiences like to see the eyes of the performer, to create that connection. Of course, there are the exceptions to the rule - for instance, the Bono's of this world with his coloured sunglasses.

Slowly Mart was able to play and la-la along with his eyes open, and without looking at what he was doing. So now it was time to introduce the lyrics into the mix.

Mart found this part surprisingly easy, as he started speaking the words to the song. As he was just speaking without a tune, this gave him less to think about. After a few attempts, he began to weave in the tune with the words. Before he knew it, he was playing guitar and singing at the same time!

Step 10: Putting it all together

Now Mart found that he had completed the first ten steps, and was ready to have his first complete run through of 'Every Rose Has Its Thorn', singing while playing guitar simultaneously.

His first ever performance of the song remains in pride of place on his iPhone, and he now regularly plays this and other songs at home when the moment takes him!

Step 11: Playing to an audience for the first time

At the point of writing this, Mart already has his first 'gig' lined up, playing a song at a friends wedding. They are still thrashing out exactly which song it will be, but needless to say, Mart is completely ecstatic at the prospect, and that he has been able to teach himself to play guitar and sing at the same time. And I was pleased for him too!

Now you can take inspiration, and do the same yourself!

Made in the USA
Monee, IL
11 May 2023

33459012R00085